麦格希 中英双语阅读文库

人生品质故事集
不要恶作剧

【美】阿妮塔·利姆(Anita Lim) ● 主编

张琳琳 ● 译

麦格希中英双语阅读文库编委会 ● 编

全国百佳图书出版单位
吉林出版集团股份有限公司

图书在版编目（CIP）数据

人生品质故事集. 不要恶作剧 /(美) 阿妮塔·利姆 (Anita Lim) 主编；张琳琳译；麦格希中英双语阅读文库编委会编. — 2版. — 长春：吉林出版集团股份有限公司, 2018.3（2022.1重印）
（麦格希中英双语阅读文库）
ISBN 978-7-5581-4763-0

Ⅰ.①人… Ⅱ.①阿… ②张… ③麦… Ⅲ.①英语—汉语—对照读物②儿童故事—作品集—世界 Ⅳ.①H319.4：Ⅰ

中国版本图书馆CIP数据核字(2018)第046445号

人生品质故事集　不要恶作剧

编：	麦格希中英双语阅读文库编委会
插　　画：	齐　航　李延霞
责任编辑：	欧阳鹏
封面设计：	冯冯翼
开　　本：	660mm×960mm　1/16
字　　数：	167千字
印　　张：	9.25
版　　次：	2018年3月第2版
印　　次：	2022年1月第2次印刷
出　　版：	吉林出版集团股份有限公司
发　　行：	吉林出版集团外语教育有限公司
地　　址：	长春市福祉大路5788号龙腾国际大厦B座7层
	邮编：130011
电　　话：	总编办：0431-81629929
	发行部：0431-81629927　0431-81629921(Fax)
印　　刷：	北京一鑫印务有限责任公司

ISBN 978-7-5581-4763-0　　　定价：35.00元
版权所有　　侵权必究　　举报电话：0431-86012683

前言 PREFACE

　　英国思想家培根说过：阅读使人深刻。阅读的真正目的是获取信息，开拓视野和陶冶情操。从语言学习的角度来说，学习语言若没有大量阅读就如隔靴搔痒，因为阅读中的语言是最丰富、最灵活、最具表现力、最符合生活情景的，同时读物中的情节、故事引人入胜，进而能充分调动读者的阅读兴趣，培养读者的文学修养，至此，语言的学习水到渠成。

　　"麦格希中英双语阅读文库"在世界范围内选材，涉及科普、社会文化、文学名著、传奇故事、成长励志等多个系列，充分满足英语学习者课外阅读之所需，在阅读中学习英语、提高能力。

　　◎难度适中

　　本套图书充分照顾读者的英语学习阶段和水平，从读者的阅读兴趣出发，以难易适中的英语语言为立足点，选材精心、编排合理。

◎精品荟萃

本套图书注重经典阅读与实用阅读并举。既包含国内外脍炙人口、耳熟能详的美文，又包含科普、人文、故事、励志类等多学科的精彩文章。

◎功能实用

本套图书充分体现了双语阅读的功能和优势，充分考虑到读者课外阅读的方便，超出核心词表的词汇均出现在使其意义明显的语境之中，并标注释义。

鉴于编者水平有限，凡不周之处，谬误之处，皆欢迎批评教正。

我们真心地希望本套图书承载的文化知识和英语阅读的策略对提高读者的英语著作欣赏水平和英语运用能力有所裨益。

丛书编委会

Contents

A Kind Act
助人为乐 ·························· 1

Catch Me If You Can
捉迷藏 ·························· 19

Keep Not What's Not Yours
拾金不昧 ·························· 39

Stop Playing Tricks
不要恶作剧 ·························· 58

Please Save Me
救人 ·························· 76

Don't Rob the Blind
善待盲人 ·························· 95

Be Careful of Strangers
小心陌生人 ·························· 112

A Kind Act

助人为乐

QUALITY LIFE STORIES 1

James and Ali like to play football. Football is their favourite game. They play in the field near their school. They can walk there.

    favourite *adj.*
    特别喜爱的

They start playing when the sun is not so hot. After a game, they go home to do their homework.

    start *v.* 开始；着手

They are nice and helpful boys. They help their friends in trouble.

    trouble *n.* 困难；问题

They are in the same class, Class Year

    杰姆斯和阿里喜欢踢足球。足球是他们最喜爱的运动。他们通常会走着去学校附近的足球场踢球。

    他们在太阳还不太热的时候，就开始踢。踢完足球，他们就回家写作业。

    这两个男孩心地善良，乐于助人。他们帮助有困难的朋友。

    他们在同一个年级——二年级。老师非常喜欢他们，这两个男

◆ A KIND ACT

Two. Their teacher likes them very much. The two boys always offer to carry their teacher's exercise books to her car.

exercise *n.* 练习；

They also offer to clean the blackboard. James is in charge of changing the pictures on the notice board. He changes them every week.

in charge of 负责

James and Ali are kicking the ball in the field. After an hour, they decide to go for a drink at a drink stall.

decide *v.* 决定； 下决心

孩总是主动帮老师把作业本送到车上。

他们也会主动擦黑板。杰姆斯负责更换公告栏的图片。他每星期更换一次。

杰姆斯和阿里在球场踢球。一小时后，他们决定去饮料摊喝一杯。

QUALITY LIFE STORIES 1

James tells Ali, "I will take my schoolbag from the locker. I will meet you at Uncle Soon's drink stall."

locker *n.* 寄存柜

stall *n.* 货摊

The two boys walk to Uncle Soon's stall. Uncle Soon greets them.

"Hi, boys! How are you this afternoon?"

They then order their favourite coffee. To them, Uncle Soon's coffee is the best.

They love to see Uncle Soon pouring the coffee from one glass to the other.

pour *v.* 斟；倒

杰姆斯对阿里说："我去储物柜拿书包，然后我们就去苏恩大叔饮料摊。"

他们个走到苏恩大叔的饮料摊。苏恩大叔和他们打招呼：

"嗨，孩子们！今天下午过得怎么样？"

他们点了自己喜欢的咖啡。对他们来说，苏恩大叔煮的咖啡是最美味的。

他们喜欢看苏恩大叔把咖啡从一个杯子倒入另一个杯子里。

◆ A KIND ACT

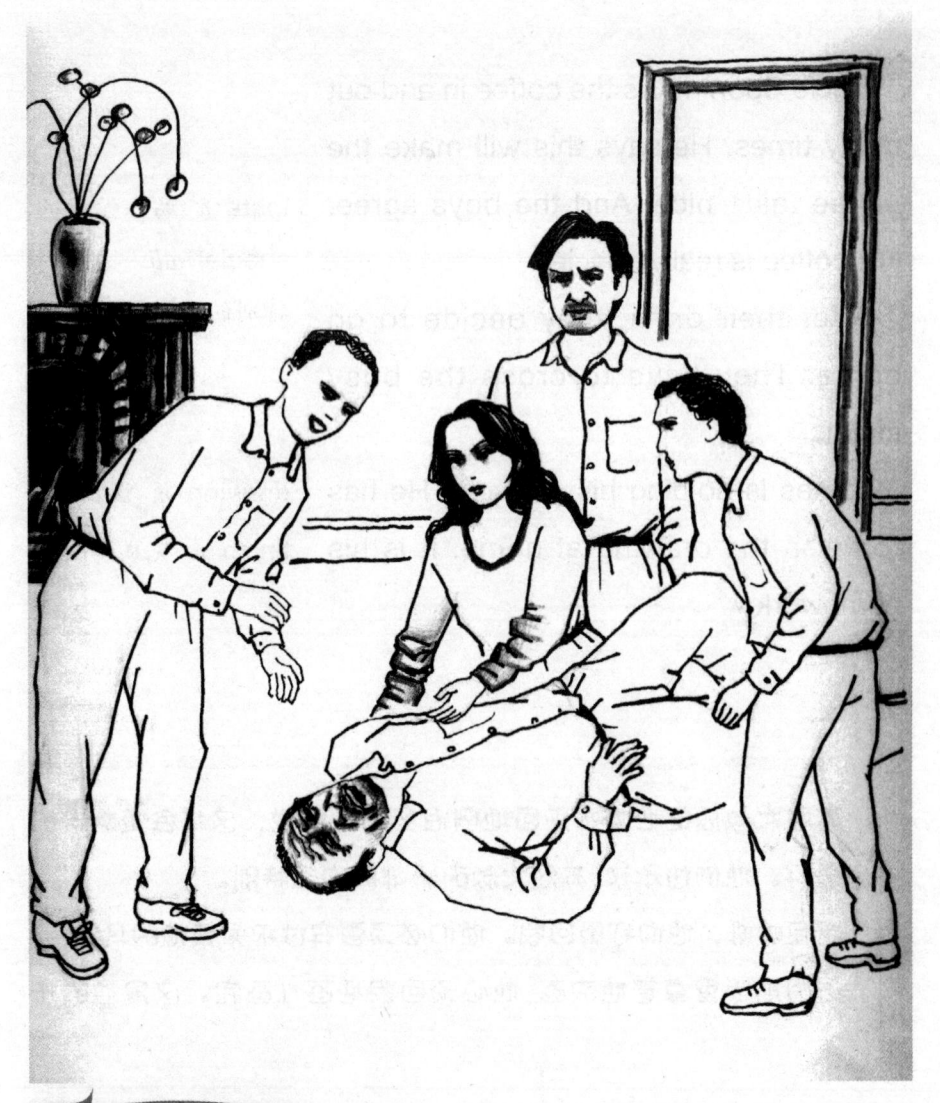

名人名言

The best man stumbles.

伟人也有犯错时。

QUALITY LIFE STORIES 1

Uncle Soon pours the coffee in and out many times. He says this will make the coffee taste nice. And the boys agree. His coffee is really special.

taste *v.* 品；尝

special *adj.* 特别的；不寻常的

After their drink, they decide to go home. They have to cross the busy street.

James is holding his drawing. He has to finish the drawing at home. It is his homework.

drawing *n.* 图画

finish *v.* 完成

苏恩大叔总是把咖啡来回地倒很多次。他说，这样会使咖啡的味道更好。他们也承认，苏恩大叔的咖啡真的很特别。

喝完咖啡，他们打算回家。他们必须要穿过那条繁忙的马路。

杰姆斯手里拿着他的画，他必须回家把画儿画完。这是他的作业。

◆ A KIND ACT

The drawing is a tower. He loves to draw buildings.

He is thinking, "I'll finish drawing at home."

James is standing at the roadside. He is waiting to cross the road. A lady comes running down the road.

She does not see James standing there. She knocks into him. James' drawing drops on the road. James looks

tower *n.* 塔；塔楼

roadside *n.* 路边；路旁

knock *v.* 碰；撞

他画的是一座塔。他喜欢画建筑。

他正想着："我要回家把它画完。"

杰姆斯站在路边，等着过马路。一位女士沿着马路跑过来。

她没有看见站在那里的杰姆斯，撞在了他身上。杰姆斯的画儿掉在了马路上。杰姆斯看着他的画。

QUALITY LIFE STORIES 1

at his drawing.

Ali also sees the drawing on the road. He walks to where James is standing.

The lady sees James' drawing all dirty on the ground.

She says, "I'm so sorry. I did not see you."

James says, "It's all right."

Ali looks at the lady. She is crying! He wonders why she is crying.

dirty *adj.* 肮脏的；污秽的

wonder *v.* 想知道

阿里也看着马路上的画。他走到杰姆斯跟前。

那位女士看着杰姆斯的画掉到了地上，全都弄脏了。

她说道："对不起，我没看见你。"

杰姆斯说，"没关系。"

阿里看了一眼这位女士。她在哭！他很想知道她为什么哭。

◆ A KIND ACT

The lady says quickly, "It's my father. He is at home. He has a heart attack!"

And she continues, "I'm looking for a taxi. The taxis will not stop."

James and Ali know the lady's father must go to hospital. The lady looks worried.

Ali quickly says, "I am waiting for my father. I will phone him to come now."

The lady replies, "Oh, thank you so

attack *n.* 发作；侵袭

continue *v.* 继续做；不停地干

worried *adj.* 担心的；担忧的

reply *v.* 回答；回复

女士快速答道："因为我父亲。他在家里，心脏病突然发作了！"

她继续说道："我在找出租车，可是出租车都不停。"

杰姆斯和阿里知道这位女士的父亲必须马上去医院。女士看起来很焦急。

阿里马上说："我在等爸爸。我现在就打电话让他过来。"

女士答道："哦，真是太感谢你了。"

QUALITY LIFE STORIES 1

much."

Ali quickly phones his father with the lady's handphone. He asks his father to come now. He tells his father about the man's heart attack.

James then runs to the lady's house. The old man is lying on the floor.

The lady runs to her father. She says, "He's still alive. I must get him to the gate. Can you help me?"

handphone *n.*
手机；移动电话

lie *v.* 躺；平躺

alive *adj.* 活着的；
有生气的

阿里立刻用女士的手机给爸爸打电话。他让爸爸马上过来。他告诉爸爸有人心脏病发作了。

然后，杰姆斯跑到女士家。老人正躺在地上。

女士跑到她父亲跟前，说："他还活着，我必须把他弄到大门口。你能帮我一下吗？"

James helps her to get the old man up to his feet.

Ali's father is at the gate. He comes into the house to help the lady and James. They manage to carry the old man to the car. Then, Ali's father drives quickly to the hospital.

The car reaches the hospital in ten minutes. The hospital attendants are waiting with a stretcher. They carry the

manage v. 完成（困难的事）

drive v. 驾驶；开车

attendant n. 护理者

stretcher n. 担架

杰姆斯帮她把老人扶起来。

阿里的爸爸来到了大门口，他走进屋里协助女士和杰姆斯把老人抬上了车。之后，阿里的父亲开车赶往医院。

十分钟后，他们赶到了医院。医院的救护人员已经准备好担架在那里等着了。他们把老人抬进医院。

QUALITY LIFE STORIES 1

old man into the hospital.

Ali's father, Ali and James wait downstairs. A while later, the lady comes downstairs. She thanks them for helping her.

downstairs *adv.*
在楼下；往楼下

Ali's father replies, "We are happy to help. I am Azman. This is my son, Ali, and his friend, James."

The lady says, "And I am Doris Tan." She shakes their hands.

shake *v.* 握手

阿里和爸爸还有杰姆斯等在楼下。过了一会儿，女士从楼上走了下来。她感谢他们给予的帮助。

阿里的爸爸说："我们很高兴能够帮上忙。我是阿兹曼。这是我的儿子阿里，还有他的朋友杰姆斯。"

女士说，"我叫多丽丝·谭。"她与他们一一握手。

♦ A KIND ACT

She then adds, "I really must thank you all for your kind act. You help me and my father a lot."

Ali's father asks Doris, "Do you need me to send you back to your house."

The lady says, "Thank you so much."

When the car reaches her gate, she gets down from the car.

She says, "I will phone you to tell you about my father."

add *v.* 补充说

send *v.* 送

然后她又说:"我很感谢你们的帮助。你们帮了我和父亲很多。"

阿里的父亲问多丽丝:"需要我送你回家吗?"

女士说,"谢谢。"

车子开到了她家门口时,她从车上下来。

她说:"我会打电话给你,告诉你我父亲的病情。"

QUALITY LIFE STORIES 1

Ali and James can see she is feeling better now. They are happy to help her.

Their parents teach them to help people.

They always say, "We will try to help people." This time, they help the lady and her father.

That night, Ali's father tells Ali's mother about the old man. Ali's mother is happy Ali is quick in asking his father to help the

| feel *v.* 觉得；感到 |
| try to 设法；尽力 |

阿里和杰姆斯看到她现在好多了。他们很高兴能帮助她。

他们的父母告诉他们要帮助别人。

他们总是说，"我们会尽力帮助他人。"这一次，他们帮助了这位女士和她的父亲。

那天晚上，阿里的爸爸把帮助老人的事告诉了阿里的妈妈。阿里的妈妈觉得很欣慰，因为阿里及时地通知爸爸去帮助女士。她总是教孩子们要帮助别人。

◆ A KIND ACT

名人名言

The darkest hour is nearest the dawn.

黎明前的黑暗。

QUALITY LIFE STORIES 1

lady. She always teaches her children to help others.

She says, "It's good you help the old man. That's the right thing to do."

In James' house, he looks at his dirty drawing that night. He cannot hand in his homework tomorrow.

He also tells his parents about Doris and her father.

James' father says, "Good, James. We

right *adj.*
正确的；正当的

hand in 提交；呈送

她说："你能帮助老人，这很好。这是应该做的事。"

晚上，杰姆斯在家里看着弄脏了的那幅画。明天，他交不上作业了。

他也跟父母讲述了多丽丝和她父亲的事。

杰姆斯的爸爸说："好样的，杰姆斯。我们很高兴你能帮助生病的老人。"

◆ A KIND ACT

are happy you help an old man in pain."

The next morning, James tells his art teacher he cannot hand in his drawing homework.

His teacher asks, "Why can't you?"

So, James tells her about the old man.

His teacher says, "It's right to help other people, especially sick people."

She says he can do the drawing in

especially *adv.*
尤其；格外

第二天早上，杰姆斯告诉他的美术老师，他不能按时上交绘画作业。

老师问他："你为什么交不上作业？"

于是，杰姆斯把帮助老人的事告诉了她。

老师说："帮助他人是对的，尤其是病人。"

她说他可以在那天的课堂上把画儿画完。

QUALITY LIFE STORIES I

class that day.

A week later, Ali's father gets a phone call from Doris. Her father is getting better.

She says, "I want to thank you all. Can I meet you all for dinner tonight? We will meet at Jake's Seafood Café."

tonight *adv.* 在今晚
seafood *n.* 海味

They are happy to hear the old man is recovering. An hour later, they are enjoying their dinner at the café.

recover *v.* 康复；痊愈

一个星期后，阿里的父亲接到了多丽丝打来的电话。得知她的父亲已经痊愈了。

她说，"我想感谢你们所有人。我可以邀请你们今晚共进晚餐吗？我们在杰克的海鲜餐馆见。"

他们听到老人康复的消息很高兴。一个小时后，他们一起在餐馆享受着他们的晚餐。

Catch Me If You Can

捉迷藏

QUALITY LIFE STORIES 1

The playground in Marble Garden is a popular place with the children. It is safe for them to play. One part of the playground has swings and see-saws.

Many children go there and play. Their mothers watch them play on the swings and see-saws. They usually bring their children there in the evening.

Hamid and Hassan like to play games on the playground with the other boys.

marble *n.* 大理石
popular *adj.* 受喜爱的；受欢迎的
swing *n.* 秋千

大理石花园的游乐场是孩子们最喜爱的地方。孩子们在那里玩耍很安全。游乐场的一角有秋千和跷跷板。

许多孩子去那里玩。妈妈们看着他们荡秋千和玩跷跷板。晚上，她们常常带着孩子来这里。

哈米德和哈桑喜欢在游戏场跟其他的男孩子玩游戏。他们在游

They play on the other part of the playground.

This part is an open field. But, the back part of it has some bushes.

bush *n.* 灌木（丛）

Hamid and the boys try not to play near the bushes. The boys like to play a game. The game is the Blind Man's Bluff.

bluff *n.* 唬人；虚张声势的做法

Usually, six will play the game. One of them is the blind man. The others tie a handkerchief or scarf round his head.

handkerchief *n.* 手帕

乐场的另一边玩。

这边是一片开阔地。但是，在这片地的后面是灌木丛。

哈米德和男孩们会尽量不在灌木丛附近玩。孩子们很喜欢玩一个游戏。游戏的名字叫"捉迷藏"。

通常，玩这个游戏的有六个人。其中一个人扮盲人。其他人把

QUALITY LIFE STORIES 1

Then, they spin him around a few times. Now blind-folded, he has to look for the others.

The boys usually play the game for an hour or so. The loser has to give each one of the players a sweet or a bun.

The boys gather at the playground. They want to play Blind Man's Bluff. They are talking and laughing.

spin *v.*
（使）快速旋转；转动

bun *n.* 小圆甜蛋糕；
小圆甜饼

laugh *v.* 笑；发笑

手帕或者围巾绕在他的头上。然后，他们让他转上几圈。他不得不蒙着眼睛，寻找别人。

这个游戏孩子们通常会玩一个小时左右。输了的人要给其他孩子每人一块糖或是一块小糕点。

男孩儿们聚集在游乐场。他们要玩捉迷藏。他们说着笑着。

◆ CATCH ME IF YOU CAN

Hamid is about to start the game. Hassan is to be the blind man. At that moment, Razak comes running and asks to join in.

Razak is a simple, friendly boy. He is also the easy-to-bully type. He looks much younger than nine years old.

Razak is not one of them. The group of six boys usually does not allow other boys to join in.

Razak looks at Hamid and says,

join *v.* 加入；参加

simple *adj.* 简单的

allow *v.* 允许；准许

哈米德打算开始游戏了。哈桑扮盲人。就在这时，拉扎克跑过来，想和他们一起玩。

拉扎克是一个单纯的、友好的男孩。同时他也是容易欺负的类型。他看起来根本不到九岁。

拉扎克不属于他们的圈子。六个男孩的小团体通常不允许其他男孩加入。

拉扎克看着哈米德说："请让我跟你们一起玩吧！"

QUALITY LIFE STORIES 1

"Please let me join in the game."

Hamid looks at him. He asks, "Where is your mother?"

Razak replies, "She is at the shop. She will not be back yet."

Hamid looks at the small-sized boy. He can be very naughty at times. He is thinking, "I will play a trick on Razak."

So, he looks at Razak and says with a laugh, "All right. But, you have to be the

naughty *adj.*
顽皮的；淘气的

哈米德看了看他，问："你妈妈在哪儿呢？"

拉扎克回答："她在商店。她还不会回来。"

哈米德看着这个矮小的男孩。他有时很调皮。他正在想着："我要捉弄一下拉扎克。"

于是，他看看拉扎克，笑着说："好。可你得扮盲人。"

blind man."

Hassan looks surprised. Why does Hamid let an outsider be the blind man?

Then, Hassan sees a naughty look in Hamid's eyes. He pulls Hamid aside and asks, "What are you up to?"

Hamid tells Hassan, "I want to play a trick on him."

Hassan asks him, "How?"

Hamid says, "I want to lead him to the

surprised *adj.*
惊奇的；

outsider *n.* 外人；
   局外人

lead *v.* 引导

哈桑很惊讶。为什么哈米德会让局外人扮盲人呢？

然后，哈桑看到了哈米德眼中狡黠的神情。他将哈米德拉到一边问道："你这是要做什么？"

哈米德告诉哈桑："我想捉弄他。"

哈桑问他，"怎么捉弄？"

哈米德说："我打算把他领到灌木丛。他会想抓住我。这时，

QUALITY LIFE STORIES 1

名人名言

The devil knows many things because he is old.

老马识途。

◆ CATCH ME IF YOU CAN

bushes. He tries to catch me. He will flip over and fall on the bushes."

Hassan says, "That's dangerous. The bushes have so many thorns. They will cut him."

And Hamid says, "It's fun to see the thorns prick him."

Hassan says, "Don't do that. His mother will scold you."

Then, Hassan reminds Hamid the rule

| flip *v.* （使）快速翻转；迅速翻动 |
| thorn *n.* 刺；荆棘 |
| prick *v.* 扎；刺 |
| scold *v.* 训斥；责骂 |

他就会滑倒，跌进灌木丛。"

哈桑说："那样很危险。灌木丛中荆棘丛生。他会被割伤的。"

哈米德说："看着他被刺儿扎不是很有趣嘛。"

哈桑说："别那么做。他妈妈会骂你的。"

接着，哈桑提醒哈米德捉迷藏的游戏规则。游戏的规则是不要

QUALITY LIFE STORIES 1

of the Blind Man's Game. The rule of the game is never to lead the blind man to places that will cause physical hurt.

But, Hamid is eager to start the game. So, Hassan passes the handkerchief to Hamid. He then ties the handkerchief round Razak's head.

He spins Razak around a few times. Razak is starting to feel dizzy. Hamid then takes Razak round the playground.

physical *adj.*
身体的；肉体的

eager *adj.* 渴望的；
热切的

dizzy *adj.*
头晕目眩的；眩晕的

把"盲人"领到容易受伤的地方。

可是，哈米德急切地宣布游戏开始了。因此，哈桑只好把手帕交给哈米德。他把手帕系在了拉扎克的头上。

他领着拉扎克转了几圈。拉扎克感觉头晕了。哈米德又领着拉扎克在游乐场绕了一圈。其他人都跟在后面。

◆ CATCH ME IF YOU CAN

The others follow.

They start shouting, "Over here, Razak! Over here!"

Everyone is laughing. One boy even goes up as near as possible to Razak to tease him.

Hamid runs back to join the group. He joins in the shouting and teasing. He is almost within Razak's outstretched hands.

shout *v.* 高呼；大叫

tease *v.* 取笑；戏弄

outstretched *adj.* 张开的；伸展的

他们开始大声叫喊："在这里，拉扎克！在这里！"

每个人都在笑。一个男孩甚至上前靠近拉扎克逗弄他。

哈米德跑到后面加入到那些男孩中。他跟他们一起喊叫，戏弄拉扎克。拉扎克几乎一伸手，就能抓到他。

He whispers to Razak, "Razak, catch me if you can. Follow my voice."

The others shout too, "Catch me if you can!"

Razak is walking with his eyes covered. He nods and giggles, "Hamid, wait till I catch you!"

He follows the sound of Hamid's voice. Hamid is leading him towards the bushes! Come, come!

follow *v.* 跟随；跟着

giggle *v.* 傻笑；咯咯地笑

他在拉扎克耳边说："拉扎克，来抓我啊。顺着我的声音。"

其他人也都喊："有本事就来抓我！"

拉扎克蒙着眼睛向前走。他点着头笑着说："哈米德，等着，我来抓你了！"

他随着哈米德的声音走。哈米德正把他领向灌木丛！来啊，来啊！

◆ CATCH ME IF YOU CAN

The others follow. They stop in their tracks. They stare at Hamid and then at one another with surprise.

track *n.* 痕迹；踪迹

The boys now realize Hamid is leading Razak to the bushes! They know it is dangerous to go to the bushes.

realize *v.* 意识到；认识到

Hamid is breaking the rule of the game. Razak will get hurt!

Razak continues to follow Hamid's voice. Hassan is feeling scared. He

scared *adj.* 害怕的；担心的

其他人跟在后面。他们停下不走了。他们盯着哈米德看，吃惊地互相看着。

男孩儿们现在意识到哈米德正把拉扎克领向灌木丛！他们知道去灌木丛是很危险的。

哈米德在破坏游戏规则。拉扎克会受伤的！

拉扎克继续循着哈米德的声音往前走。哈桑很害怕。他希望拉扎克不要再走了。

QUALITY LIFE STORIES 1

hopes Razak will stop walking.

Hamid is backing towards the bushes. He does not know a ladder is lying on the ground. It is behind him. He will trip on it.

Hassan can see it.

He wants to shout, "Hamid, look out!" But he cannot.

So, Hamid trips over the ladder. He falls flat on the ground. Razak falls on top of him!

ladder *n.* 梯子

哈米德朝着灌木丛方向后退。他不知道身后的地上放着的梯子会将他绊倒。

哈桑看到了。

他想喊："哈米德，小心！"可他喊不出来。

因此，哈米德绊在了梯子上。他直挺挺地跌倒在地。拉扎克趴在了他身上！

The next thing he is shouting, "Oh, no! Ouch! Razak, get off me!"

Razak also trips over the ladder. But, he falls on top of Hamid. So, he is not hurt. The thorns go into Hamid's arms and legs. Razak, who is on top of Hamid, pulls down the handkerchief.

By then, the others reach them. And they stand around and laugh.

Hamid and Razak look funny. The boys

top *n.* 上部；顶部

pull down 拉下来；
推翻

他紧接着喊道："哦，不！哎哟！拉扎克，快从我身上下来！"

拉扎克也绊在了梯子上。但是，他摔在了哈米德的身上。因此，他并没有受伤。荆棘刺入哈米德的胳膊和大腿。拉扎克躺在哈米德的身上，拉下手帕。

这时，其他人都赶到了他们身边。他们站在一旁笑。

哈米德和拉扎克看起来很滑稽。男孩儿们帮忙拉起拉扎克和哈

QUALITY LIFE STORIES 1

help to pull Razak and Hamid up.

Hamid has cuts and scratches on his hands and legs.

Hassan says, "Hamid, you are badly hurt. You better go home."

Hamid looks at his hands and legs.

Looking at the others and Razak, Hamid says he is sorry.

He apologizes, "I'm sorry for breaking the rule of the game."

scratch *n.* 擦伤划痕

badly *adv.* 严重地；厉害地

apologize *v.* 道歉；谢罪

米德。

哈米德的手上和腿上到处都是割伤和划伤的伤口。哈桑说："哈米德，你伤得很严重。你最好回家。"

哈米德看着他的手和腿。

看着其他人和拉扎克，哈米德说他很抱歉。

他向所有人道歉："对不起，我破坏了游戏规则。"

◆ CATCH ME IF YOU CAN

Hassan and the other boys nod their heads.

They all agree that the rule of the game is good for them. In a game, nobody must get hurt.

Hamid goes home. His mother sees his cuts and scratches.

She brings him to a clinic immediately. The doctor gives him an injection.

Of course, Hamid learns his lesson.

clinic *n.* 小诊所
injection *n.* 注射；注射剂
of course 当然；一定

哈桑和其他男孩儿都点头同意。

他们都认同，游戏的规则对他们有益。在游戏中，一定不能有人受伤。

哈米德回到家。他的母亲看到了他割破和划破的伤口。

立即把他带到诊所。医生给他打了针。

当然，哈米德得到了教训。就是永远不要打破游戏规则，游戏

QUALITY LIFE STORIES 1

名人名言

The early bird catches the worm.

早起的鸟儿有虫吃。

◆ CATCH ME IF YOU CAN

That is never to break the rules of the Blind Man's Bluff game. Nobody must get hurt during the game.

The next week, Razak goes with his mother to the playground. Razak dares not go and join Hamid's group.

He is scared of another trick. Hamid walks over to talk to Razak's mother. He tells her Razak can play with them.

Hamid promises her. Nobody will get

promise v. 保证；允诺

中一定不能有人受伤。

第二周，拉扎克和妈妈一起去了游乐场。拉扎克不敢去和哈米德他们玩。

他害怕再被捉弄。哈米德走到拉扎克妈妈身边。他告诉她拉扎克可以和他们一起玩。

哈米德答应她。没有人会受伤。他们将遵守游戏规则。

QUALITY LIFE STORIES 1

hurt. They will follow the rules of the game.

So Razak happily runs to join the group. They boys are happy Razak is one of them.

Hamid, Hassan and the other boys continue to play the Blind Man's Bluff on the playground.

But they always play by the rules of the game. Nobody must get hurt during the game.

during *prep.*
在……的期间

因此拉扎克兴高采烈地跑来加入这个团体。男孩儿们对于拉扎克的加入感到很高兴。

哈米德、哈桑和其他男孩继续在游乐场玩捉迷藏。

但他们一直遵守游戏规则。游戏中一定不能有人受伤。

Keep Not What's Not Yours

拾金不昧

QUALITY LIFE STORIES 1

Christine has only one brother called Tommy. So, they are close to each other. Their parents are busy working.

Their mother is a hawker. She sells chicken rice at the food court. Their father is a truck driver. Tommy has to look after his sister.

Christine is eight years old. Tommy is three years older. He loves to work at the computer. He can spend hours playing

close *adj.* 亲密的；密切的

hawker *n.* 沿街叫卖者；小贩

food court *n.* 美食广场

克里斯汀只有汤米一个哥哥。所以，他们彼此间很亲近。他们的父母总是忙于工作。

他们的母亲是一个小贩，她在美食街卖鸡肉饭。他们的父亲是卡车司机。因此，汤米不得不照看着妹妹。

克里斯汀今年八岁了。汤米比她大三岁。他喜欢玩电脑。他能一连玩上好几个小时的电脑游戏。

◆ KEEP NOT WHAT'S NOT YOURS

computer games.

He plays the games with Christine. He also loves to surf the Internet. He downloads pictures, songs and cards.

download *v.* 下载；下传

Christine learns a lot about computers from her brother. She learns how to download images and songs.

image *n.* 图像；影像

Sometimes their parents ask them, "You two can sit in front of the computer for hours. Don't you get tired?" They will

tired *adj.* 疲倦的；厌倦的

他跟克里斯汀一起打游戏。他还喜欢上网冲浪。他有时也会下载一些图片、歌曲和图卡。

克里斯汀从哥哥那里学会了很多电脑知识。她学会了如何下载图片和歌曲。

有时父母会问他们："你们两个在电脑前一坐就是好几个小时。你们不累吗？"他们永远也不会厌倦电脑的。

QUALITY LIFE STORIES 1

never get tired of the computer.

　　Christine and her brother are eating at a café. They often go there to eat. Food at the café is nice and cheap.

　　Christine is eating fried noodles. Tommy is having fish and chips. They have to share their table with another person. The café is crowded with people.

　　This person is a man in his twenties. He is eating noodle soup. After eating, he

café *n.* 咖啡馆；
　　　小餐馆

fried *adj.* 油炸的；
　　　煎炒的

share *v.* 分享；共享

crowded *adj.*
挤满了人的

　　克里斯汀和哥哥在小店里吃饭。他们经常去那里。小店里的食物又好吃又便宜。

　　克里斯汀要的是炒面。汤米吃的是鱼和薯条。小店里挤满了人，他们只好跟一个陌生人坐在一张桌上。

　　这个男人二十多岁。他正在吃汤面。吃完后，他去了洗手间。五分钟后，他出来了。接着，他走出了小店。

◆ KEEP NOT WHAT'S NOT YOURS

goes to the restroom. Five minutes later, he comes out. And he walks out of the café.

Christine sees his black sling bag on the chair. The man leaves behind his sling bag.

She quickly tells Tommy. "Tommy, the man left behind this sling bag."

Tommy looks at the sling bag. It is not very big. There seems to be something

restroom *n.* 洗手间；休息室

sling *n.* 吊带；吊索

克里斯汀看到他的黑色单肩包还在椅子上。他把单肩包落在这儿了。

她马上说："汤米，那个人把包落在了这儿。"

汤米看了看这个单肩包。不是很大，里面似乎有什么东西。他拉开包，向里面看，他看到里面有一台笔记本电脑。

QUALITY LIFE STORIES 1

inside. He unzips it to look at the inside. He sees a notebook computer inside.

| unzip v. 拉开……的拉链
| notebook n. 笔记本

　　Tommy always wants a notebook computer. But his parents tell him, "You don't need one anyway. There is a computer at home."

　　But Tommy says, "I can carry it everywhere. I can use it in my room. Christine can use the computer in the living room."

| carry v. 携带；持有

　　汤米一直想要一台笔记本电脑。但他父母总是说："家里有台式机，你根本不需要笔记本。"

　　但汤米说："我可以带着它到处走。我可以在房间里用笔记本。这样，克里斯汀就可以用客厅的电脑了。"

◆ KEEP NOT WHAT'S NOT YOURS

And now, there is one inside the sling bag. He wants it! He tells Christine, "Sis, let's take the bag home. It has a notebook. I can have a notebook now!"

Christine stares at her brother. "Can we? What if the owner comes back and looks for it?"

Tommy stands up. He quickly takes her hand with his left hand. And his right hand is holding the sling bag. Then, he

stare *v.* 盯着看；凝视

look for 寻找；寻求

hold *v.* 握住；抓住

现在，单肩包里面就有一台。他想拥有它！他告诉克里斯汀："妹妹，我们把它带回家吧。里面有一台笔记本电脑，我现在有笔记本电脑啦！"

克里斯汀盯着哥哥问："我们可以这样做吗？如果失主回来找它怎么办？"

汤米站起来。他用左手迅速地拉起她的手，右手拎起单肩包。然后，他领着克里斯汀快速地离开了小店。

leads his sister out of the café quickly.

Outside the café, Tommy walks to his bicycle.

He quickly puts the bag into the basket on his bicycle. He tells Christine, "Get up on the bicycle now. Quickly!"

Christine does that. She looks pale. She knows they are doing a wrong thing. Tommy pedals as fast as he can down the road towards home.

pale *adj.* 苍白的；灰白的

pedal *v.* 骑(自行车)；踩板

在小店外面，汤米走到自己自行车跟前。

他急急忙忙地把包放进自行车的车筐里。他告诉克里斯汀："快点上车。"

克里斯汀赶紧上了车。她脸色苍白。她知道他们在做一件错事。汤米飞快地骑着自行车往家走。

KEEP NOT WHAT'S NOT YOURS

Back home, Tommy and Christine rush to the living room. Tommy takes out the nice notebook computer.

It is quite new. He likes it. Now he has his own notebook. But Christine tells him, "Tommy, we cannot keep this notebook. It's not ours. We must tell father about this."

Tommy says, "No, you cannot tell him. I'll hate you if you tell him."

rush v. 冲；奔

quite adv. 相当

hate v. 仇恨；憎恨

回到家里，汤米和克里斯汀急忙来到客厅。汤米从包里拿出那台漂亮的笔记本电脑。

它几乎是新的。他很喜欢。现在他有自己的笔记本电脑了。但克里斯汀告诉他："汤米，我们不能要这个笔记本，这不是我们的。我们必须把这件事告诉父亲。"

汤米说："不，你不能告诉他。如果你告诉他，我会恨你的。"

QUALITY LIFE STORIES 1

Christine does not know what to do. She does not want her brother to hate her. But, she knows keeping other people's things is wrong.

keep *v.* 保留；留下

Tommy is happily fixing it in his room. She asks him, "What will you tell father about this?"

fix *v.* 安装；固定

Tommy says quickly, "I will say a friend lends it to me to use."

lend *v.* 借给；借与

Christine is thinking, "Now you are

克里斯汀不知道该怎么办。她不想让哥哥恨她。但是，她知道拿别人的东西是不对的。

汤米高兴地把笔记本放在了他的房间。克里斯汀问他："你打算怎么向父亲解释这台笔记本？"

汤米急忙答道："我就说是我的一个朋友借给我的。"

克里斯汀想了想说："现在你又说谎了。"她知道这是不对的。

◆ KEEP NOT WHAT'S NOT YOURS

名人名言

The eye is bigger than the belly.

贪多嚼不烂。

QUALITY LIFE STORIES 1

lying too." She knows it is wrong.

Then, Christine sees three diskettes and documents inside the bag. She tells Tommy, "These belong to the owner."

Tommy looks at them. There are a few name cards. One name card shows the notebook belongs to John Kee. He is working for Key Computers Enterprise.

The next morning they go to school. On the way to school, Christine tells

lie *v.* 说谎；撒谎

diskette *n.* 软（磁）盘；塑料磁盘

belong to 属于

enterprise *n.* 公司；企业

然后，克里斯汀在单肩包里发现了三个磁盘和一些文件。她告诉汤米："这些都是失主的。"

汤米看了看包里的东西。找到了几张名片。其中一张表明：笔记本的主人是纪约翰，他在关键电脑公司上班。

第二天早上，他们去上学。在去学校的路上，克里斯汀告诉汤米："也许我们应该给失主打电话。你知道他的名字。告诉他电脑在我们这儿。"

◆ KEEP NOT WHAT'S NOT YOURS

Tommy, "Maybe, we should phone the owner. You know his name. Tell him we have his notebook"

After school, they go home quickly. They take out the name card. They phone John Kee's mobile phone.

The phone rings. A man answers the phone.

Tommy says, "You are John Kee? I am Tommy. I have your notebook. Can you

mobile phone 手机
ring *v.* 响起铃声

放学后,他们赶快回到家里。他们拿出名片,拨通了纪约翰的手机。

电话响了几声。一个男人接起了电话。

汤米说:"你是纪约翰吗?我是汤米。我检到了你的笔记本。你能过来取一下吗?"

QUALITY LIFE STORIES 1

come and get it?"

John Kee rushes to the park near Christine's house. He is very happy to get back his notebook.

get back 取回；收回

He says to Tommy, "Thank you very much. So, you and your sister like computers. Are you good at using them?"

Tommy says, "Not really. My sister and I are still learning. We have an old

really *adv.* 真正地；
实际上

纪约翰赶到了克里斯汀家附近的公园。他非常高兴能找回笔记本电脑。

他对汤米说："非常感谢。既然你和妹妹喜欢电脑。那么你们精通电脑吗？"

汤米说，"不是很精通。我和妹妹还在学。我们有一台旧电脑。我的父母买不起新的。"

computer set. My parents cannot afford to buy a new one."

And John Kee tells them, "I have an old notebook computer. I can let you use it first."

Tommy and Christine shout together, "Thank you."

John Kee continues, "You two are honest people. I want to thank you for returning my notebook."

set *n.* 家用电器

afford *v.* 承担得起

honest *adj.* 诚实的；老实的

return *v.* 归还；送回

纪约翰告诉他们："我有一台旧的笔记本电脑。你可以先用着。"

汤米和克里斯汀一起喊道："谢谢你。"

纪约翰接着说道："你们两个很诚实。我要谢谢你们归还我的笔记本。"

QUALITY LIFE STORIES 1

John Kee adds, "I will teach you how to use the notebook. You can come and see my computer equipment in my house."

They are happy to hear that. They cannot wait to go to John Kee's house.

"First, we will go back to your house. Then, I will talk to your parents."

They go back to Christine's house. He tells Christine's parents, "I want to give

equipment *n.* 设备；装备

cannot wait to 迫不及待做某事

纪约翰还说："我会教你们如何使用笔记本电脑。你们可以来我家，参观我的电脑设备。"

听到这，他们很高兴。他们已迫不及待地要去纪约翰的家看看。

"首先，我们要回你们家去。然后，我会跟你们的父母谈谈。"

他们回到克里斯汀家。他告诉克里斯汀的父母："我想给他们一台旧笔记本电脑，还想教他们学电脑。"

◆ KEEP NOT WHAT'S NOT YOURS

them an old notebook. I will also teach them more about computers."

Christine's father looks at the man. John Kee seems all right. He is serious about his work.

serious *adj.* 严肃的

So, Christine's father follows Christine and Tommy to John Kee's house. His house has a big computer room.

At his house, he shows them his computers, notebooks and other machines like the printer and burner. He

show *v.* 拿给……看

burner *n.* 燃烧器

克里斯汀的父亲打量着这个人。纪约翰看上去很不错。他对待工作很认真。

因此，克里斯汀的父亲跟着克里斯汀和汤米来到纪约翰的家里。他家有一间大的电脑房。

在他家，他领着他们参观了自己的电脑、笔记本电脑和其他设备，如"打印机和燃烧器"等。他告诉他们："作为一个平面设计师，所有这些设备都是必需的。"

QUALITY LIFE STORIES 1

名人名言

The finest diamond must be cut.

玉不琢，不成器。

KEEP NOT WHAT'S NOT YOURS

explains to them, "As a graphic designer, I need all these."

Tommy is amazed to see the complete computer equipment. John Kee explains the equipment to them.

John Kee is saying he will teach Tommy and Christine how to use them.

Tommy is thinking it is good to be honest. Now, he can learn about computers. One day, he will be a computer engineer or graphic designer.

graphic *adj.*
绘画的；绘图的

designer *n.*
设计师；设计者

amazed *adj.*
惊奇的；吃惊的

complete *adj.*
完整的；全部的

汤米惊讶地看着这么完整的电脑设备。纪约翰向他们展示了这些设备的功能。

纪约翰说他会教汤米和克里斯汀如何使用它们。

汤米想，做诚实的人真好。现在，他可以学电脑了。总有一天，他会成为一名电脑工程师或者平面设计师的。

Stop Playing Tricks

不要恶作剧

STOP PLAYING TRICKS

Gopal is a naughty boy. He is always playing tricks in class. His classmates do not like him.

His two brothers also keep away from him. They are Ravi and Kannan. They will not play with him. He uses their pencils without asking them for permission. Then, he breaks them.

So, Gopal is quite lonely. His brothers do not want to talk to him. In school, his

keep away 不接近；远离

permission n. 同意；允许

break v. 折断

lonely adj. 孤独的；独单的

戈帕尔是一个调皮的男孩。他总是捉弄班上的同学，同学们都不喜欢他。

他的两个兄弟拉维和卡纳安也总是远远地躲着他。他们不跟他一起玩。他总是擅自使用他们的铅笔。用完后，就把铅笔折断。

所以，戈帕尔很孤独。他的兄弟不跟他说话。在学校，同学们也不想跟他在一起。他总是一个人在食堂吃饭。

QUALITY LIFE STORIES 1

classmates do not want to be with him. In the canteen, he eats alone at the table.

His mother tells his father, "Nobody wants to be near our son, Gopal."

His father says, "He asks for it. Why can't he be a nicer boy?"

His mother then says, "I know Gopal is naughty at times. But, I don't like to see him so lonely."

His father then says, "He has to

canteen *n.* 食堂；小卖部

ask for 自找麻烦；自讨苦吃

他的母亲告诉他的父亲："没有人愿意靠近我们的儿子戈帕尔。"

他的父亲说："他自找的。为什么他就不能做一个好孩子呢？"

他的母亲接着说："我知道戈帕尔有时很调皮。但是，我不想看到他这么孤独。"

他的父亲说："那他就得改改了。他必须停止嘲笑朋友和同

change then. He has to stop making fun of his friends and classmates. He has to stop playing tricks on others. I hope he will stop soon."

His mother agrees with his father. But, Gopal does not want to change. He continues to play tricks on others.

He likes to see his classmates get angry. The angrier they get, the louder he laughs. Poor Gopal! He cannot see this is

change *v.* 改变；变革

loud *adv.* 大声地
poor *adj.* 可怜的；
不幸的

学。他必须停止捉弄别人。我希望他很快就能改好。"

他的母亲很赞同。但是，戈帕尔并不想改。他继续捉弄着别人。

他喜欢看到同学们生气的样子。他们越生气，他笑得就越大

QUALITY LIFE STORIES 1

not good for him. People stay away from him.

One day, Gopal wants to play a trick on his classmate, Charles. Charles is the smartest boy in class. And Gopal dislikes him.

So far, Gopal fails to play tricks on him. He plays tricks on many boys and girls in his class. They get very angry with him.

But, Charles does not know about

dislike *v.* 不喜欢；厌恶

fail *v.* 未能……；未做……

声。可怜的戈帕尔！他意识不到这样不好。大家都躲着他。

一天，戈帕尔想捉弄他的同学查尔斯。查尔斯是班上最聪明的孩子。戈帕尔不喜欢他。

可到目前为止，戈帕尔一直没能捉弄到他。他已经捉弄了班上的许多男生和女生。他们都很生他的气。

但是，查尔斯并不知道戈帕尔要捉弄他的事。在他看来，戈帕

Gopal and his tricks. To him, Gopal is a noisy boy. He talks too much in class.

The teachers always scold him. He never finishes his homework. He always forgets to bring his books.

Charles likes to mix with his clever classmates. They study hard. They do all their homework. The teachers like him.

The teachers tell their class to study hard. Studying is important.

noisy *adj.* 吵嚷的；喧闹的

mix *v.* 交往；相处

important *adj.* 重要的；有价值的

尔是一个吵闹的男孩，他在班上太能说话了。

老师们总是责备他。他总是写不完作业，总是忘带书。

查尔斯喜欢和聪明的同学待在一起。他们学习刻苦，按时完成作业。老师们都喜欢查尔斯。

老师告诉同学们要努力学习。学习很重要。

In class, they must pay attention. They must not play in class. They can play during recess.

Miss Anna Lee, their class teacher, always tells other teachers, "Charles is a good boy. He is also a good pupil. Why can't Gopal be like him?"

On hearing this, the other teachers agree with her. They know about Gopal and his tricks.

pay attention 集中注意力；注意

recess *n.* 休息；休会

pupil *n.* 小学生；学生

在课堂上，他们必须注意听讲。他们不能在课上玩。他们可以在课间休息时再玩。

他们的班主任李安娜老师总是对其他的任课老师说："查尔斯是好孩子，也是好学生。为什么戈帕尔不能像他一样呢？"

对于这些话，其他教师都很赞同。他们知道戈帕尔和他的那些恶作剧。

◆ STOP PLAYING TRICKS

Gopal knows all the teachers like Charles. He does not like this. He does not like Charles.

This is his plan. He will put glue on Charles' chair during recess. After recess, Charles sits on his chair. He will get glue on his pants! That will be funny.

So, during recess, Gopal leaves the canteen earlier. He walks quickly to the classroom. He is holding a tube of strong

glue *n.* 胶；胶水

pants *n.* 裤子；长裤

strong *adj.* 有力的；强有力的

戈帕尔知道所有的老师都喜欢查尔斯。这让他很不高兴。他不喜欢查尔斯。

于是他想出个主意。他要在午休时把胶水涂在查尔斯的椅子上。等到午休结束，查尔斯就会坐到椅子上。到时候，他的裤子就会沾满胶水啦！肯定很好笑。

于是，在午休时，戈帕尔早早地离开餐厅。他拿着一管儿强力

QUALITY LIFE STORIES 1

glue.

In the classroom, he walks to Charles' chair. And he presses some glue on Charles' chair.

press *v.* 压挤

The school bell is ringing. The pupils go back to class. They all go back to their desks.

bell *n.* 铃；钟

Gopal is thinking happily, "Charles will get glue on his pants. He thinks he is so clever. Ha! Ha!"

clever *adj.* 聪明的；机灵的

胶快步走到教室。

在教室，他来到查尔斯的座位，把一些胶水挤在了他的椅子上。

上课铃响了。学生们走回教室，回到自己的座位。

戈帕尔正高兴地想："查尔斯会把胶水弄到裤子上。他觉得自己太聪明了。哈！哈！"

◆ STOP PLAYING TRICKS

But, when he gets back to the classroom, he does not see Charles sitting on his chair. He asks Mary who sits next to him, "Where is Charles?"

Mary says, "Charles has to go home. He is not feeling well."

Gopal is not feeling happy about this. He is thinking, "So, Charles escapes my trick this time. Tomorrow, I will do it to him."

next to 紧靠…旁边…；在…近旁

escape *v.* 逃脱；免除

但是，当他回到教室，他发现查尔斯没在座位上。他问查尔斯的同桌玛丽："查尔斯上哪儿去了？"

玛丽说："查尔斯回家了。他不舒服。"

戈帕尔对此很不高兴。他想："这次查尔斯就这样逃过了我的恶作剧。明天，我还要捉弄他。"

QUALITY LIFE STORIES 1

名人名言

The fox knew too much, that's how he lost his tail.

机关算尽太聪明，反误了卿卿性命。

◆ STOP PLAYING TRICKS

Looking at his desk, he does not see his teacher, Miss Anna Lee, walking to Charles' desk.

Miss Anna Lee is looking at her class. She is teaching them drawing. She asks the class to take out their drawing paper and brushes.

She sees Charles' chair. It is empty. So, she walks to Charles' chair.

Miss Lee is going to sit on Charles'

drawing *n.* 绘图；描图

take out 拿出；取出

brush *n.* 画笔；毛笔

empty *adj.* 空的

看着自己的课桌，戈帕尔没有看到李安娜老师正朝查尔斯的座位走去。

李安娜老师正看着她的学生们。她教他们绘画。她让学生们把画纸和画笔拿出来。

她看到查尔斯的座位是空的。于是，她走到查尔斯的椅子旁。

李老师打算坐在查尔斯的椅子上。戈帕尔看到他的老师要坐在

QUALITY LIFE STORIES 1

chair. Gopal now sees his teacher about to sit down on the chair. He is feeling scared. What can he do? He cannot tell her not to sit on Charles' chair.

scared *adj.* 害怕的；恐惧的

He can only think, "Teacher, please don't sit on the chair."

Miss Lee sits down on Charles' chair. She takes out her drawing paper and brush. She wants to show her class how to draw a tree.

sit down
(使)坐下；(使)就座

那把椅子上了。他很害怕。他该怎么办？他无法告诉她不要坐查尔斯的椅子。

他只能在心里想："老师，请千万不要坐那把椅子。"

李老师坐在了查尔斯的椅子上。她拿出画纸和画笔。她想教学生们如何画树。

"Look here, class. To draw a tree..." She feels something sticky on her skirt. She stops talking and looks at her skirt.

sticky *adj.*
黏的；涂有黏性物质的

She looks down at the chair now. It has strong glue. And there is a lot of it.

She is feeling very angry. She looks at her class. She knows one of them does it. This is a trick on Charles. She will find out who did it.

find out 找出；查明

She guesses it must be Gopal.

guess *v.* 猜测；推测

"看这里，孩子们。画树……"她感觉有东西粘在了她的裙子上。她停下来，看了一眼她的裙子。

她又朝下面看了一眼椅子。她看到了强力胶。椅子上有很多强力胶。

她感到非常生气。她看了看学生们。她知道这件事是他们中的一个人做的。这是一个要捉弄查尔斯的恶作剧。她会找出是谁干的。

她猜一定是戈帕尔。

QUALITY LIFE STORIES 1

Miss Lee asks angrily, "Who put the glue on this chair?"

The class look at their teacher. They can see the glue on her skirt. Nobody says anything.

| look at 看；朝……看 |

Miss Lee then says, "That's a very naughty thing to do."

The class look at one another.

Tuck Heng, the class monitor, says, "I think it is Gopal. He is the one who put

| monitor *n.* 班长 |

李老师生气地问："是谁把胶水涂到了这把椅子上？"

学生们看着他们的老师。他们看到了粘在她裙子上的胶水。没有人说话。

接着，李老师说："这样做，非常淘气。"

同学们你看看我，我看看你。

班长刑塔克说："我觉得是戈帕尔干的。是他把胶水涂到了查

glue on Charles' chair. I see him come back to the classroom during recess. Only he comes back to the classroom."

Miss Lee asks Gopal, "Is this true? Are you the one?"

Everyone looks at Gopal.

The class know he is the naughty one. He always plays tricks on them.

So, they all shout, "He must be the one!"

true *adj.* 真的；真实的

尔斯的椅子上。我看到午休时他回到教室。只有他回到了教室。"

李老师问戈帕尔："他说的是真的吗？是你干的吗？"

大家都看着戈帕尔。

同学们都知道他就是那个搞恶作剧的人。他总是捉弄他们。

所以，他们异口同声地喊道："一定是他干的！"

QUALITY LIFE STORIES 1

Miss Lee asks Gopal to go to the headmaster's room. There, she tells Mr Chong about the glue.

Mr Chong talks to Gopal. He tells Gopal what he did is wrong.

Gopal feels sorry about his action. He promises to stop playing tricks on others.

From that day onwards, Gopal never plays tricks on others again. He is a nicer boy. His classmates see the change in

headmaster *n.* 校长；

action *n.* 行为；
所做的事

onwards *adv.*
从（某时）起一直

李老师让戈帕尔去校长办公室。在那里，她向庄校长讲了胶水的事。

庄校长找戈帕尔谈话。他告诉戈帕尔这样做是不对的。

戈帕尔为他的行为道了歉。他保证不会再捉弄别人了。

从那天起，戈帕尔再也没有捉弄过别人。他成了好孩子。同学们看到了他的变化。

him.

They become his friends now. He is no longer lonely.

And he thinks, "Playing tricks is silly. I will never do it again."

no longer 不再

silly *adj.* 愚蠢的；笨的

现在，大家都跟他做朋友。他再也不孤独了。

他觉得："捉弄别人很愚蠢，我再也不会这样做了。"

Please Save Me

救人

◆ PLEASE SAVE ME

Chee Meng likes the outdoor life. He joins the Sports Club and Swimming Club in school. He is active in the club activities.

He also plays many games. From playing games, he becomes a healthy boy. He makes many new friends. They play games with him.

Chee Meng lives with his parents and sister. They are members of the

outdoor *adj.*
户外的；露天的

active *adj.*
积极的；勤奋的

activity *n.* 活动

member *n.* 会员；一分子

孟憨喜欢户外活动。他参加了学校的体育俱乐部和游泳俱乐部。他积极地参加俱乐部的活动。

他做许多运动。通过这些运动，他变得健康强壮，交了很多新朋友。他们与他一起做运动。

孟憨与他的父母和妹妹生活在一起。他们都是他家附近天空俱乐部的会员。那里有一个大大的游泳池。

QUALITY LIFE STORIES 1

SKY Club near their house. It has a big swimming pool.

There, Chee Meng learns swimming. He goes swimming with his friends. He is the best swimmer among them. He can easily swim ten laps at one time.

Every Sunday, he teaches swimming lessons at the SKY Club. The children enjoy their swimming lessons.

They always ask him, "Chee Meng,

pool *n.* 水池；池塘

swimmer *n.* 游泳的人

lap *n.* 一圈；游泳全程

在那里，孟憨学会了游泳。他和朋友们一起去游泳。他是他们中游得最好的。他可以很轻松地一口气儿游上十圈。

每个星期日，他都在天空俱乐部教游泳课。孩子们喜欢他上的游泳课。

他们总是问他："孟憨，教我们怎么游泳。"他教他们如何在

show us how to do this stroke." He teaches them how to float in water. He teaches them to breathe in the water.

His advice to them is, "Learn to float first. Keep your body above the water. Kick your legs properly. Use your arms properly. Then, you can swim without getting tired."

He often tells his friends how important swimming is. A good swimmer can save

stroke *n.* 游泳姿势；
   游泳方式
float *v.* 浮动；漂浮
breathe *v.* 呼吸
kick *v.* 踢（腿）

水上漂浮。他教他们如何在水里呼吸。

  他给他们的建议是："学游泳，要先学会漂浮。让你的身体浮在水面上。适时地踢动你的腿。适当地划动你的手臂。然后，你游起来就不会感到累了。"

  他经常告诉他的朋友学会游泳很重要。游泳高手可以拯救生命。

QUALITY LIFE STORIES 1

lives.

Many people cannot swim. Yet they go to the river or sea. Many drown.

He tells them, "If there is a flood, we must be able to swim. When the boat overturns, it is useful to know how to swim." He talks so much about swimming. They call him 'Swimmer Meng.'

One Saturday, Chee Meng's parents

drown *v.* 淹死；溺死

flood *n.* 洪水；大水

overturn *v.* 倾覆；翻转

很多人即使不会游泳，也会去河边或海边。会有许多人淹死。

他对他们说："如果发生了洪灾，我们必须要会游泳。一旦船翻了，会游泳就很重要了。"他讲了很多关于游泳的事，人们都管他叫"孟泳"。

一个星期六，孟憨的父母组织大家去海滩游玩。他们经常去镇子附近的海滩。

◆ PLEASE SAVE ME

organize a trip to the beach. They often go to the beach near their town.

Five families join the trip. All of them can go in the van.

Before noon, Chee Meng and the others arrive at the beach. His father books five chalets. After checking into their chalets, they want to go swimming.

Chee Meng's mother says, "Chee Meng, I have to prepare some

organize *v.* 组织；安排

van *n.* 面包车

chalet *n.* 小屋；瑞士的农舍

一家五口都参加了这次海滩之旅。他们坐进了一辆小客车。

孟葱和家人在中午前抵达了海滩。他的父亲在一家小旅馆预定了五个人的住处。办完入住手续后，他们想去游泳。

孟葱的母亲说："孟葱，我得准备一些三明治。你看好妹妹。"

QUALITY LIFE STORIES 1

sandwiches. You look after your sister."

They all walk to the beach. Many people are swimming or playing in the sea. The water is cool. The girls do not want to swim. They cannot swim well. The waves are too strong for them.

So the girls walk on the beach collecting seashells and corals. Their little brothers and sisters are building sandcastles. Their fathers are relaxing

wave *n.* 波；波浪

coral *n.* 珊瑚；珊瑚虫

sandcastle *n.* 沙塔；沙堡

他们走到海滩。很多人都在海中游泳或戏水。水有点凉。女孩子们不想游泳。她们游得不好。对她们来说，海浪太大了。

所以女孩子们就在沙滩上捡贝壳和珊瑚。小弟弟和小妹妹们在海滩上堆沙堡。爸爸们躺在阴凉的树下悠闲地看着杂志。

◆ PLEASE SAVE ME

名人名言

The greatest talkers are always least doers.

语言的巨人总是行动的矮子。

QUALITY LIFE STORIES 1

under the shady tree and reading their magazines.

At sunset, it is time for dinner. They have a barbecue.

Chee Meng, his family and their friends also make a campfire on the beach.

The night is full of fun. They play games and even dance under the moonlight sky. It is like a beach party.

Everyone has a good time. It is so nice

shady *adj.* 多阴的；成荫的

barbecue *n.* 烤肉；户外烤肉餐

campfire *n.* 营火；篝火

日落时，该吃晚餐了。他们在海滩烧烤。

孟憨和家人及朋友也在海滩点起了篝火。

夜晚有着无尽的乐趣。他们在海滩上玩耍，甚至在月光下跳起了舞。就像是一场热闹的海滩派对。

每个人都玩得很开心。与家人和朋友在一起很美好。

◆ PLEASE SAVE ME

to be with family members and good friends.

The next morning, they wake up early. The whole morning, they go trekking in the jungle. They study some unusual plant species.

Chee Meng has a camera. He takes many pictures of the trees and plants. He will print the pictures and keeps them in his album.

wake *v.* 醒；醒来
trek *v.* （尤指在山中）远足；徒步旅行
jungle *n.* 丛林；密林
species *n.* 物种

第二天早上，他们很早就起来了。整个上午，他们都在丛林中跋涉。他们研究着一些不寻常的植物物种。

孟慜有台照相机。他拍了许多树木和植物的照片。他要打印出这些照片，放在他的相册里。

QUALITY LIFE STORIES 1

Chee Meng loves nature. He prefers to live in the countryside. The air is fresh in the countryside. He can look at trees, plants and flowers.

In the city, he misses the greenery. He sees only tall buildings and traffic jams.

He is thinking, "I would love to stay here on weekends."

After lunch, Chee Meng and the boys decide to have a relaxing afternoon

nature *n.* 大自然；自然界

countryside *n.* 农村；乡下

greenery *n.* 绿色植物；草木

traffic jam 交通阻塞；塞车

孟憩热爱大自然。他喜欢住在乡下。这里空气清新，他可以看到树木，植物和花卉。

而在城市里，他看不见绿色。他看到的只有高高的大楼和拥挤的交通。

他在想："我以后每个周末都要来这里。"

午饭后，孟憩和男孩子们决定在树荫下过一个轻松的下午。

◆ PLEASE SAVE ME

under a shady tree.

David asks Chee Meng, "How are your squash lessons? I hear you are playing squash."

squash *n.* 墙网球；壁球

Chee Meng answers, "It's a tiring game. But, it's good exercise. Why don't you join me?"

The boys decide to relax. Mark plays his guitar. The other boys sing and clap their hands.

relax *v.* 休息；放松

clap *v.* 拍（手）；鼓（掌）

戴维问孟蕙："你的壁球学得怎么样了？我听说你在玩壁球。"

孟蕙回答："这项运动很累人，但却是很好的锻炼。你们为什么不跟我一起玩呢？"

男孩们决定轻松一下。马克弹起了吉他。其他的男孩和着吉他唱着歌，拍着手。

QUALITY LIFE STORIES 1

Their mothers are busy clearing away the dishes and cups. They throw the food remains in a garbage bag.

The girls prefer to take a nap in the chalets. The little ones are running and playing on the sand.

Suddenly, the group of boys hears someone shout, "Help! Help! Someone is drowning."

Chee Meng looks far out to the sea.

clear *v.* 使干净
dish *n.* 盘；碟
garbage *n.* 垃圾；废料

妈妈们正忙着收拾盘子和杯子。她们把剩下的食物扔进垃圾袋。

女孩子们在小屋里睡午觉。小孩子们在沙滩上追逐嬉戏。

突然，男孩儿们听到有人喊："救命！救命啊！有人落水了。"

孟憨向远处的海面看去，他看到一个孩子在水中挣扎。强大的

◆ PLEASE SAVE ME

He sees a child struggling in the water. The strong wave is sweeping the child away. The child is drifting in the water. He cannot swim.

Chee Meng can hear more shouts. There are no lifeguards around. The child is still in the water.

Someone is saying, "He is going to drown. Oh dear!"

The girls standing on the sand start

sweep *v.* （风、汹涌的海水等）席卷；横扫

drift *v.* 漂流；漂

lifeguard *n.* 救生员；警卫

海浪正把孩子推向大海深处。孩子漂在水上。他不会游泳。

孟葱听到了更多的喊声。海滩上没有救生员。孩子仍在水中。

有人说："天啊！他要淹死了。"

女孩子们站在沙滩上开始哭泣。她们听到喊叫后都很害怕。

QUALITY LIFE STORIES 1

名人名言

The leopard cannot change its spots.

本性难移。

◆ PLEASE SAVE ME

crying. They are all scared to hear that.

Chee Meng knows he must act fast. He is running to the sea. He swims very fast to the child. With his strong hands, he pulls the child to him.

The child's parents are standing on the sand. They are worried for their son. It is true Chee Meng is a good swimmer. But, the waves are very strong.

Chee Meng's father also runs to the

scared *adj.* 害怕的；恐惧的

pull *v.* 拉；牵

孟葱知道他必须迅速采取行动。他奔向大海，快速地向孩子游去，用他强有力的手，把孩子拉到他身边。

孩子的父母站在沙滩上。他们很担心自己的儿子。孟葱的确是个游泳好手。可海浪也非常大。

孟葱的父亲也跑向海岸。其他的男人和男孩也很快跟了上去。他们都盯着海面。

QUALITY LIFE STORIES 1

shoreline. The other men and boys soon follow him. They all look at the sea.

They see Chee Meng pulling the child against the wave. He is such a good swimmer. Then, he pulls the child to the shore. Everyone claps at his bravery.

There is a big crowd of people now. They see Chee Meng carrying the child towards the deckchair.

The child is still alive! The child's

shoreline *n.* 海岸线

shore *n.* 岸；海岸

bravery *n.* 勇敢；勇气

deckchair *n.* 躺椅；帆布躺椅

他们看到孟憨拉着孩子与海浪对抗。他真是个游泳好手。不久，他把孩子拉到岸边。大家为他的勇气报以热烈的掌声。

岸上聚了一大群人。他们看到孟憨把孩子抱到躺椅上。

这孩子还活着！孩子的父母向他跑去。他们感谢孟憨救了他们孩子的命。

◆ PLEASE SAVE ME

parents run to him. They thank Chee Meng for saving their child's life.

Everyone comes closer to look at the child on the deckchair.

In the evening, the child and his parents join Chee Meng's friends.

It is then the child's parents tell Chee Meng. "We don't know how to thank you. We would like you to take this cheque from us."

cheque *n.*
支票；空白支票

人们都围过来看望躺椅上的孩子。

到了晚上，孩子和父母来到了孟慈和他的朋友中间。

就在这时，孩子的父母对孟慈说："我们不知道该如何感谢你。我们希望你能收下这张支票。"

QUALITY LIFE STORIES 1

Chee Meng says he cannot take it. His father then tells him, "Son, it's all right. Mr Chong wants to thank you."

Uncle Bob takes pictures of Chee Meng and the child. The child knows this brave boy saves his life.

He holds Chee Meng's friend. To him, Chee Meng is a hero.

hero *n.* 英雄

After all this, everyone claps and sings, 'For he is a jolly good fellow, for he is a jolly good fellow...'

jolly *adv.* 很；非常

孟憨说他不能收。这时，父亲对他说："儿子，没关系。庄先生是想感谢你。"

鲍勃叔叔为孟憨和孩子拍了照。孩子知道这个勇敢的大哥哥救了自己的命。

他把孟憨当成了朋友。对他来说，孟憨是一个英雄。

之后，每个人都拍着手唱着歌："因为他是个很好的人，因为他是个很好的人……"

Don't Rob the Blind

善待盲人

QUALITY LIFE STORIES 1

David goes to Lee Tuition Centre for his science tuition classes. Many people walk along the busy street.

There are many beggars and blind people sitting at the corner of the street. The blind people play their guitars for the people to listen.

David likes to stand near the shop and listen to the music. One blind man can play his guitar very well. The people call

tuition *n.* 教学；讲授

science *n.* 科学；自然科学

beggar *n.* 乞丐；行乞者

戴维去李先生的补习班上科学课。繁华的街道上有很多人。

有许多乞丐和盲人坐在街角。盲人们为路人弹奏着吉他。

戴维喜欢站在商店附近听音乐。那儿有个盲人，吉他弹得很好。人们称他为"盲人音乐家。"

◆ DON'T ROB THE BLIND

him 'Blind Musician'.

He plays his guitar and sings pop songs. People like to hear him play and sing. They drop money in his large blue box.

David is standing in front of the shop again. He is waiting for his father to fetch him.

He is watching the blind musician play the guitar. He likes to hear the blind man

musician *n.* 音乐家；乐师

pop *adj.* 流行的

drop *v.* 放下；投下

fetch *v.* 去接

他弹吉他，唱流行歌曲。人们喜欢听他演奏和歌唱。他们把钱放进他蓝色的大盒子里。

戴维站在商店前面，等爸爸来接他。

他看着盲人音乐家演奏吉他。他喜欢听这个盲人唱歌。

QUALITY LIFE STORIES 1

sing.

David is thinking, "I wish I can play like him. He is blind but he is so talented."

talented *adj.*
有才能的；天资高的

The street is quiet at this time. Most people are working or are staying at home.

Then, David notices a boy moving near the blind musician.

move *v.* 移动；
搬动

David knows he is up to no good. The boy is about six years old. The boy goes

---

戴维想："真希望我能像他弹得一样好。他虽然看不见，但他很有才华。"

这个时间段儿，街道上很安静。大多数人都在上班或是待在家里。

这时，戴维注意到有个小男孩正朝着盲人音乐家走去。

戴维知道他做不出好事来。那个小男孩大约六岁的样子。小男孩走近盲人音乐家坐的地方。他悄悄地迅速地接近盲人。

◆ DON'T ROB THE BLIND

near where the blind musician is sitting. He moves very quietly and quickly.

The boy puts out his hand and grabs some dollar notes from the blue box.

grab *v.* 抓取；攫取
note *n.* 钞票；纸币

The blind musician knows it. He shouts. "Help! Help! A thief is stealing my money."

steal *v.* 偷窃；偷盗

People do not pay attention. They are in a hurry to go somewhere.

in a hurry 匆忙

Some of them cannot hear the

小男孩伸出手，从蓝盒子里抓了一把钱。

盲人音乐家察觉了。他大声叫道："来人啊。来人啊。有小偷偷我钱。"

没有人关注这件事。他们都来去匆匆。

有些人甚至都没听到喊声。车子的噪音太大了。

QUALITY LIFE STORIES 1

shouting. The noise from the traffic is loud.

    David sees this. He thinks quickly, "The thief has the blind man's money. I must do something."

    So, he moves in the direction of the thief. The thief runs past David.

    David quickly puts out his leg. The thief trips and falls on the road. His money drops on the ground.

noise *n.* 喧闹声；嘈杂声

direction *n.* 方向

thief *n.* 小偷；窃贼

    戴维看到这儿，他想："小偷拿了盲人的钱，我得做点什么。"

    因此，他朝小偷的方向走去。小偷跑过戴维身边。

    戴维迅速地伸出腿。绊倒了小偷。他跌坐在马路上，他的钱掉到了地上。

◆ DON'T ROB THE BLIND

David shouts at him, "You thief! You take a blind man's money!"

The thief looks at David. He runs away quickly before David chases him.

chase *v.* 追；追赶

David bends down and picks up the dollar notes. He then walks to the blind musician. The blind man looks sad.

bend down 俯身；屈身

He says to the blind man, "I have back your money. The thief trips and falls."

He then hands the money to the blind

戴维对他大叫："你这个小偷！你偷了盲人的钱！"

小偷看着戴维。急忙逃走了，戴维没能抓住他。

戴维弯下腰，捡起钱。然后他走到盲人音乐家跟前。盲人看起来很伤心。

他对盲人说："小偷摔倒了，我把你的钱捡回来了。"

然后，他把钱递给盲人。

QUALITY LIFE STORIES 1

名人名言

The outsider sees the most of the game.

旁观者清。

man.

The blind man puts the money in his blue box. He thanks David for getting back his money.

He says, "You are very kind. What's your name?"

David says, "I am David. What is your name?"

And the blind man replies, "I am Ah Tong. They call me Singer Ah Tong."

singer *n.* 歌手；唱歌的人

盲人把钱放到蓝色的盒子里。他感谢戴维找回了他的钱。

他说："你人真好。你叫什么名字？"

戴维回答："我叫戴维。您叫什么名字？"

盲人回答："我叫阿唐。他们叫我歌手阿唐。"

QUALITY LIFE STORIES 1

David is so happy to know Ah Tong. They start talking.

Ah Tong knows a lot about pop songs. He plays by listening to songs. Then, he plays the guitar and sings the songs. He can sing very well.

David sees his father's car coming down the road.

He says, "I have to go now. Tomorrow, I will come and talk to you. We can talk

listen *v.* 听；留神听

戴维很高兴能认识阿唐。他们开始聊天。

阿唐很了解流行歌曲。他通过听歌学习歌曲。然后，他边弹吉他边唱歌。他唱得很好。

戴维看到爸爸的车开过来了。

他说："我要走了。明天，我再来和你聊天。我们可以谈论歌曲。"

◆ DON'T ROB THE BLIND

more about songs."

Ah Tong is waving goodbye to him. David walks to his father's car. He is happy he has a new friend now.

In the car, David tells his father about Ah Tong. He describes the young thief stealing money from Ah Tong.

describe *v.* 叙述

David's father says, "That's wrong. We should do our best to help the blind people and not rob them. They need our

rob *v.* 偷取；盗去

阿唐和他挥手告别。戴维朝爸爸的车走了过去。他很高兴交了个新朋友。

在车上，戴维给爸爸讲了阿唐的事。他告诉爸爸有个小孩儿偷阿唐钱。

戴维的爸爸说："这样是不对的。我们应尽全力去帮助盲人而不是欺负他们。他们需要我们的帮助。"

QUALITY LIFE STORIES 1

help."

The next day, David is waiting for his father to fetch him. His tuition class is just over. He is looking for the young thief.

look for 寻找；寻求

Five minutes later, the young thief comes walking down the road. He is carrying a schoolbag. He is swinging his schoolbag.

swing *v.* 使摇摆；使摇晃

David calls out to him, "Hey, you!"

第二天，戴维在等着爸爸来接他。补习班刚下课。他在找那个偷钱的小孩。

五分钟后，那个偷钱的小孩走过来了。他拿着一个书包，用手来回悠荡着。

戴维朝他喊道："喂，你过来！"

◆ DON'T ROB THE BLIND

The boy looks at David. He says, "Why are you calling me? I am not stealing."

David says, "It's wrong to steal. Don't you know that?"

David continues, "We should help the blind people. We cannot take their things. The blind people cannot see. They need us to help them."

The boy hears this. He looks ashamed. He wants to run away.

ashamed *adj.*
羞愧的；惭愧的

那小男孩看着戴维。他说："你叫我干什么？我又没偷钱。"

戴维说，"偷东西是不对的。难道你不知道吗？"

戴维接着说："我们应该帮助盲人，不能拿他们的东西。盲人看不见，他们需要我们的帮助。"

小男孩听了这些话，感到很羞愧。他想跑开。

QUALITY LIFE STORIES 1

David says, "Good. Now, you go and apologize to the blind musician. His name is Ah Tong."

The boy is not willing to go. He just stands there.

David says, "You have to say sorry to him. That is the right thing to do."

David holds his hand and says, "Come, let's walk to Ah Tong. He wants to be your friend."

apologize *v.* 道歉；认错

willing *adj.* 情愿的；自愿的

戴维说："好了。现在，你去向那个盲人音乐家道歉。他叫阿唐。"

小男孩不愿意去，站在那里不动。

戴维说："你必须向他道歉。那是你应该做的事。"

戴维牵着他的手说："来吧，我们去找阿唐。他会愿意跟你做朋友的。"

◆ DON'T ROB THE BLIND

名人名言

The pot calls the kettle black.

五十步笑百步。

QUALITY LIFE STORIES 1

The boy follows David to where Ah Tong is sitting. Ah Tong can hear them coming to him.

David calls out, "Ah Tong. Someone wants to say something to you."

Ah Tong is waiting for the boy to talk.

The boy says, "I'm sorry Ah Tong, for taking your money. I will not do it again." He looks ashamed. He looks down at the road.

follow *v.*
跟随；跟着……去

look down 朝下看

小男孩跟着戴维来到阿唐身边。阿唐听到了他们的脚步。

戴维说："阿唐。有人有话要对你说。"

阿唐等着小男孩开口。

小男孩说："对不起，我昨天拿了你的钱。我不会再那么做了。"他很惭愧地低下了头。

◆ DON'T ROB THE BLIND

Ah Tong asks him "What's your name?"
The boy says softly, "Ah Hock."
Ah Hock then asks, "Will you teach me to play the guitar?"
Ah Tong says, "Of course. Come and sit down here."
From that day, the three become good friends. Ah Hock learns to be kind to blind people.

softly *adv.* 温和地；轻柔地

of course 自然；毫无疑问

阿唐问他："你叫什么名字？"
小男孩轻声说，"我叫阿福。"
随后阿福问："你会教我弹吉他吗？"
阿唐回答："当然。来，坐到这边来。"
从那天开始，三个人成了好朋友。阿福学会了善待盲人。

Be Careful of Strangers

小心陌生人

◆ BE CAREFUL OF STRANGERS

Other people always tell me, "Listen to your father. He knows best."

This is the best advice anyone can give me.

But, like many boys, I dislike listening to my father sometimes.

I do not do things the way he wants me to do. I want to do things my way. See what happened to me when I did.

My mother said, "Peter, listen to us.

advice n. 建议；劝告

dislike v. 不喜欢；厌恶

happen v. 发生；引起

别人总是告诉我，"听你父亲的。他最明白。"

这是任何人都可以给我的好建议。

但是，像许多男孩一样，我有时不喜欢听父亲的。

我不愿意按照他希望的方式做事，我想按自己方式做事。让我们来看看，我这样做了之后的结果吧。

母亲对我说："彼得，听我们的吧。我正在浪费时间说服你。

QUALITY LIFE STORIES 1

I am wasting my time advising you. We ask you to study. You play your guitar."

"We advise you to go to bed early. You need the sleep. But, you play computer games till midnight. You don't do what we say."

midnight *n.* 午夜；子夜

My father added, "Wait till one day when something happens. And I will tell you, I told you so."

add *v.* 补充说

I listened to those words many times.

我们让你学习，你偏要弹吉他。"

"我们建议你早睡，你需要睡眠。但是，你熬夜玩电脑游戏。你根本就不听我们的话。"

父亲补充道："等到有一天，事情真的发生了。我会对你说，我早就告诉过你。"

这些话我听了很多次了。

◆ BE CAREFUL OF STRANGERS

Of course, I tell myself, "Parents worry too much."

They give too much advice. Many times, the advice is not necessary. So, I thought. And I continued playing my guitar until midnight.

necessary *adj.*
必要的；必不可少的

My father also advised me not to talk to strangers.

stranger *n.* 陌生人；
陌生事物

He said, "Peter, don't think that you are a boy they will not hurt you. They can

---

当然，我告诉自己，"父母的担心太多余了。"

他们给了我太多的忠告。很多时候，这些建议根本就没有必要。所以，我有自己的想法。我继续弹着我的吉他，一直弹到午夜。

我的父亲也告诫我不要和陌生人说话。

他说："彼得，不要认为你是一个男孩，他们就不会伤害你。

rob you. They can beat you up. They can cheat you. So, just be careful."

Good advice. But I was thinking, "It won't happen to me. I am a big boy."

That day, my father was supposed to take me to the shop to buy a computer. My old computer was giving me problems.

But, my father phoned to say he could not come home that afternoon.

beat *v.* 打；猛击

cheat *v.* 骗取；欺诈

be supposed to 应该

他们可以抢走你的东西。他们可以把你胖揍一顿。他们可以欺骗你。所以，要小心。"

建议是好建议。可我想："这些事都不会发生在我身上，我是一个大男孩了。"

这一天，我父亲本来要带我去商店买电脑。我的旧电脑老是给我找麻烦。

但是，父亲打来电话说他那天下午不能回家了。

BE CAREFUL OF STRANGERS

He told me to withdraw the money from an ATM machine. Then, I was to go to the shop and wait for my elder sister, Lucy.

Lucy would phone my father to come to the shop. Lucy is four years older than me. My parents always ask her to look after me.

They do not worry so much about her. They always say, "Be more like your

withdraw *v.*
提，取（款）

machine *n.* 机器

elder *adj.*
年龄较大的；年长的

他告诉我从自动取款机取钱。然后，去商店等我姐姐露西。

露西会打电话给父亲让他去商店。露西比我大四岁。我的父母总是让她照顾我。

他们总是对她很放心。他们总是说："多像你姐姐学学。她很

QUALITY LIFE STORIES 1

sister. She is careful unlike you."

I would think I am bigger than her. I can look after her instead.

On the phone, my father said clearly. "Be careful. There are many robberies and crimes. Don't talk to any stranger outside the bank"

He added, "Just use your ATM card and withdraw the money. Then, walk away quickly."

| unlike *prep.* |
| 不像；和……不同 |
| instead *adv.* |
| 反而；却 |
| robbery *n.* 抢劫案； |
| 盗窃案 |
| crime *n.* 犯罪行为 |

谨慎，不像你。"

我宁愿自己比她大，由我来照顾她。

在电话里，父亲说得清楚："要小心！发生过许多抢劫和犯罪事件。不要在银行外面和任何陌生人说话。"

他补充说，"记住用提款卡取出现金。然后，赶紧离开。"

◆ BE CAREFUL OF STRANGERS

名人名言

There are two sides to every question.

问题皆有两面。

QUALITY LIFE STORIES 1

I laughed and said, "No, I won't, Dad."

I was thinking. He was worrying too much.

I felt I was a big boy. I could look after myself. What could a stranger do to me?

I am tall for my age. No stranger can kidnap me. No man can beat me up or cheat or rob me. I am a match for any man. That is not smart thinking, I realized later.

kidnap *v.* 绑架；诱拐
match *n.* 对手；敌手

我笑着说，"哦，我不会有事的，爸爸。"

我的想法是，他的担心太多余了。

我觉得我是个大男孩了。我能照顾好自己。陌生人能对我做什么呢？

我的个子很高，远远高过同龄人。没有陌生人能绑架我。没有人能揍我，欺骗或打劫我。我对任何人来说都是个强劲的对手。我后来才意识到，这个想法很愚蠢。

◆ BE CAREFUL OF STRANGERS

In my mind, I imagined the stranger attacking me. I was picturing myself as a strong and brave boy.

I would sweep him down, send him away with a few swift blows. And he would never come near me again.

To me, it was that simple.

I took out my ATM card from my drawer. Usually, my mother does not let me use the ATM card. She keeps the

attack *v.* 袭击；打击

sweep *v.* 使（手臂）挥动

swift *adj.* 快速移动的

在我的脑海中，我想象着陌生人攻击我。我想象着自己是一个坚强勇敢的男孩。

我会把他打翻在地，一阵拳脚，就能把他打跑。他永远也别想再靠近我。

对我来说，就这么容易。

我从抽屉里拿出提款卡。通常，母亲不让我用提款卡。她总是把提款卡放在抽屉里。

QUALITY LIFE STORIES 1

card inside the drawer.

But, that day, she was not in. And my father asked me to take it out to use it.

But, he did say I was to be very careful with the money. He reminded me to wear the pouch around my waist.

I put the ATM card into my wallet. Then, I took a rest and read a comic magazine.

Reading comics is my favourite

remind *v.* 提醒

pouch *n.* 小袋；烟草袋

waist *n.* 腰；腰部

comic *n.* 连环漫画

但是，那天，她不在家。父亲叫我拿出来用。

但是，他确实说了，让我拿着钱小心点。他提醒我要把钱包系在腰上。

我把提款卡放进钱包。然后，休息了一会儿，看了会儿漫画杂志。

阅读漫画是我最喜欢的消遣。所以，我用零花钱买了很多漫画杂志。

pastime. So, I use my pocket money to buy comic magazines.

The shelves in my room are full of comic magazines. I like nothing better than to take them down and read them again and again. Sometimes, I lend them to my cousins and friends.

At three o'clock, I decided to go to the bank.

I live near the bank. It took me just five

pastime *n.* 娱乐；消遣

shelf *n.* 架；书架

cousin *n.* 堂（表）兄弟姊妹

bank *n.* 银行

我房间的书架上全是漫画杂志。我最喜欢把它们取下来，一遍又一遍地看。有时，我把它们借给我堂妹和朋友。

三点钟的时候，我决定去银行。

银行就在附近。我只花了五分钟就走到了银行。

QUALITY LIFE STORIES 1

minutes to walk to the bank.

    I reached the bank. There was a queue inside the ATM machine room.

queue *n.* 排队；
等候行列

    I used to see my father join the queue. So, I did the same thing.

    While waiting, I looked around at the people. They looked all right to me. There was no need to worry at all.

    My father reminded me of my PIN number on the phone. I entered the

PIN *n.* 个人识别编号；个人专用暗码

enter *v.* 进入

到了银行。自动取款机前，排了一条长长的队。

我常看父亲去排队。所以，我也这样做了。

排队等的时候，我打量了一下周围的人。他们看起来没有什么问题。根本没有必要担心。

父亲打电话提醒我，注意保护好个人识别密码。我走进自动提

room. There, I was standing at the ATM machine.

Following what my father always did, I looked all around me first. I had to make sure nobody was watching me press my numbers. Then, I pressed the six numbers.

I wrote it on my palm. Then, I rubbed the numbers away.

I did not have to wait for long. The sum

palm *n.* 手掌

rub *v.* 擦掉；磨去

sum *n.* 合计；总计

款机室，站到自动取款机前。

像父亲经常做得那样，我先看了看周围。确信没人偷看我输入密码。然后，我按下了六位密码。

我把它写在了手掌上。然后，把它擦掉了。

我不需要等太久。3000美元就从机器中吐了出来。

QUALITY LIFE STORIES 1

名人名言

There is kindness to be found everywhere.

人间处处有温情。

◆ BE CAREFUL OF STRANGERS

of $3000 came out of the machine.

I took the money and tucked it safely inside my pouch.

tuck *v.* 把……塞进；
把……放置好

Then, I walked quickly out of the ATM machine room.

I was thinking, "Now, I will walk to the computer shop and wait for Lucy. I can get my computer today."

Just outside the room, I felt someone tapping my shoulders.

shoulder *n.* 肩膀；
肩部

我拿了钱，把它安全地放进了钱包里。

然后，我快步走出了自动取款机室。

我想着：“现在，我要去电脑店等露西。我今天就可以有新电脑了。”

刚走到外面，我感到有人拍了一下我的肩膀。

QUALITY LIFE STORIES 1

It was a man. I heard his voice.

He was asking me, "Excuse me, did you drop this...?"

I turned around. A thin smoke swirled before my face. I breathed in, not knowing what it was. I immediately felt dizzy and weak. I could not think clearly any more.

I only heard a soft voice saying, "Follow me."

swirl *v.* 打旋；旋动

weak *adj.* 无力的；
脆弱的

是一个男人。我听到他的声音。

他问我："请问，这是你掉的……？"

我转过身。薄薄的烟雾飘到我脸上。我深深地吸了口气，不知道这是什么。我立刻感到头晕无力。我有些意识不清了。

我只听到一个柔和的声音说："跟我来。"

BE CAREFUL OF STRANGERS

So, I followed him. My mind did not seem to be mine any more.

I walked behind the man. He was not tall or short.

I got into his car. I had a good look of his face. He started his car engine. He pushed his face towards mine. Then, I knew nothing.

I woke up. I saw I was lying on the ground in a dark alley. Where was this

mine *pron.* 属于我的

engine *n.* 引擎；发动机

alley *n.* 小巷；胡同

于是，我跟着他。我的意识似乎不再受我控制了。

我跟在他身后。他不高也不矮。

我上了他的车。我仔细看了看他的脸。他发动了汽车。他把他的脸转向我。然后，我就什么都不知道了。

醒过来的时候，我发现自己躺在地上，在一条黑暗的小巷子

QUALITY LIFE STORIES 1

place? Slowly, I got up. I saw my pouch was empty.

All the money had gone! I started to cry.

At the same time, I realized my father was right. He said, "Be careful of strangers."

I phoned my father. He came to fetch me from the alley.

He took me to the police station.

police station *n.* 警局

里。这是哪儿？我慢慢地站了起来。我发现我的钱包是空的。

所有的钱都不见了！我开始哭泣。

此时，我意识到父亲是对的。他告诉我：“小心陌生人。”

我打电话给父亲。他把我从巷子里接出来。

他把我带到警察局。

◆ BE CAREFUL OF STRANGERS

The policeman was very kind. He asked me gently, "Can you recognize the man?"

I told him I saw the man's face clearly in the car. He had a long scar on the right side of his face.

The policeman told me, "The stranger hypnotized you. So, you could not think clearly. You followed what he said. It happened to many others. There is

gently *adv.* 温和地；
文雅地

recognize *v.* 识别；
辨认出

scar *n.* 疤；伤痕

hypnotize *v.*
对……施催眠术

警察很和蔼。他温和地问我："你能认出他吗？"

我告诉他在车里我看清了他的脸。他右边的脸上有一条长长的疤。

警察告诉我："那个陌生人催眠了你。所以，你才会不受意识控制。你会听他的。这种案子发生过很多起了。有一帮人专做这

QUALITY LIFE STORIES 1

a gang of people doing this. We are keeping a lookout for them."

My father and I were shocked to hear all that.

The policeman continued, "Last month alone, there were twenty such cases in the city. It happened to teenagers and children. These children and teenagers were alone. They stepped out of the bank. The robbers were waiting outside."

gang *n.* 一组；一群
lookout *n.* 监视；注意
shock *v.* 感到震惊；受到震动

个。我们正在密切监视他们。"

听到这些我和父亲很震惊。

警察接着又说，"单单上个月，这个城市就发生了二十起这样的案子。都发生在青少年和儿童身上。这些儿童和青少年都是独自一人。他们走出银行。抢劫犯在外面等着。"

◆ BE CAREFUL OF STRANGERS

I was shocked to hear that.

He added, "They did the same thing to them. They would say, 'Excuse me...' And a thin smoke would swirl before the face."

He continued, "And the victims would listen to the robbers' words. Many got into the robbers' cars. The robbers took their money."

I learnt a painful lesson. From that day

thin *adj.* 淡的；稀薄的

victim *n.* 受害人；遭难者

word *n.* 话；言词

painful *adj.* 痛苦的；难受的

我吃了一惊。

他补充说，"他们作案手段相同。他们会说："请问……"，薄薄的烟雾就会飘到他们脸上。"

他继续说，"受害者会听抢劫犯的话。许多孩子上了抢劫犯的车，他们的钱就这样被抢走了。"

我得到了惨痛的教训。从那天起，我一直很小心。

QUALITY LIFE STORIES 1

onwards, I was very careful.

Strangers talked to me. I would not turn around. I would not shake their hands. I would not follow them. I would not get into their cars.

My father is right. Be careful of strangers.

My father gave me money again to buy the new computer. This time, he went with me to the shop.

turn around
（使）转身；（使）转向

陌生人跟我说话，我不回头。我不同他们握手。我不跟着他们走。也不上他们的车。

父亲是对的。小心陌生人。

父亲又给了我买新电脑的钱。这一次，他和我一起去了商店。

BE CAREFUL OF STRANGERS

He also learnt a lesson. That is not to let a ten-year-old boy withdraw money at a bank. Bad men may harm the boy.

harm *v.* 伤害；危害

It is safer for parents to go to the shop with their children.

After my lesson, I told my friends to be careful too. I advised my cousin sisters not to go near strangers. They are not to talk to strangers.

If someone behind them says, "Excuse

他也得到了一个教训。就是不要让一个十岁的男孩一个人在银行取钱。坏人也许会伤害孩子。

父母陪同孩子一起去商店更安全。

有了我的前车之鉴。我告诉朋友们一定要小心。我劝堂妹们不要接近陌生人，不要和陌生人说话。

如果听到有人在他们背后说，"请问……"不要转身。

QUALITY LIFE STORIES 1

名人名言

There is no place like home.

金窝银窝不如咱的狗窝。

BE CAREFUL OF STRANGERS

me..." they are not to turn around.

The girls listen to my advice. They are scared of strange men talking to them.

After that day, I noticed the people around me. I learn to be more careful when I walk in quiet areas.

area *n.* 区域；范围

In fact, I stay away from these places. We cannot stop bad men from harming us. But, we can be more careful in our movements.

movement *n.* 动作；举止

她们听了我的建议，很害怕跟她们说话的陌生人。

那天过后，我留意身边的人。我学会在僻静的地方要更加当心。

事实上，我总是远离这种地方。我们不能阻止坏人伤害我们。但是，我们可以更谨慎。

QUALITY LIFE STORIES 1

I try to give the advice to the other boys. They like to go out till late at night.

One day, I got a phone call from the police station.

The same policeman spoke to me. "Peter, can you come to the police headquarters? We need you to identify the robber."

I told him I would gladly do so. I wanted to help them catch the robber.

headquarters *n.* 总署；总部

identify *v.* 辨认；识别

gladly *adv.* 乐意地；高兴地

我也给了其他的男孩同样的建议。他们老想在外面玩到深夜。

一天，我接到了一个从警察局打来的电话。

还是那个警察，他对我说："彼得，你能到警察局来一趟吗？我们需要你辨认抢劫犯。"

我告诉他，我很乐意这么做。我想帮助他们抓住抢劫犯。这样的人应该被逮捕。

◆ BE CAREFUL OF STRANGERS

Such people must be arrested.

 My father came home. I told him about the phone call from the police. He said I was a brave boy to agree to do it.

 He added, "I am proud of you, son."

 That night, I was feeling happy to be able to do my part to help to prevent more robberies.

 The next day, we went to the police headquarters. Through the glass door, I

arrest *v.* 逮捕

proud *adj.* 自豪的；骄傲的

able *adj.* 有能力的
prevent *v.* 阻止；防止

 父亲回到家。我跟他讲了警察打来的那个电话。他很同意我这样做，这样做很勇敢。

 他补充道："我为你感到骄傲，儿子。"

 那天晚上，我感到很高兴能够尽我的责任，去防止更多的抢劫案发生。

 第二天，我们去了警察局。透过玻璃门，我看到了他。我立刻

QUALITY LIFE STORIES 1

saw him. I recognized him at once.

That was the same robber who robbed me of my money. I nodded my head. The police knew this was the robber.

Then, I walked out happily. I did my part to help the police.

My father always reads in the newspapers. Young teenagers and children get harmed.

newspaper *n.* 报纸

就认出了他。

就是那个抢了我钱的抢劫犯。我点点头。警察知道他就是那个抢劫犯。

然后，我开心地走了出来。我尽了我的一份力去帮助警察。

父亲总是在报纸上看到，青少年和儿童受到伤害。

◆ BE CAREFUL OF STRANGERS

After reading this, he will tell me. There are bad people in the city. They kidnap children and babies. They lie to children and cheat them. They even kill children and teenagers.

So, we have to be more careful of these people.

baby	n. 婴儿；婴孩
even	adv. 甚至；连

每次看到，他就会告诉我。在这个城市里有坏人。他们绑架儿童和婴儿。他们对孩子撒谎并欺骗他们。他们甚至杀害儿童和青少年。

因此，我们必须小心这些人。